PENSHAW AND SHINEY ROW Then & Now

by Lena Cooper

Royalties from this book will go to charity.

First published in 2010 by

Summerhill Books
PO Box 1210
Newcastle-upon-Tyne
NE99 4AH

www.summerhillbooks.co.uk

Email: andrew_clark@hotmail.co.uk

ISBN: 978-1-906721-28-2

Printed by CVN Print Ltd, Maxwell Street, South Shields

Printed by: CVN Print, Maxwell Street, South Shields

Contents

Introduction

The villages of Penshaw and Shiney Row have a long and proud history. This book is a glimpse of that history using old postcards, photographs, illustrations and memories. The book is a 'then and now' and there are many old photographs alongside modern views that show how much the two communities have changed over the years.

Throughout the book I share my memories of living and working in the area as well as my family connections. I talk about the days of poss tubs for washing – always done on a Monday – and of the importance of coal in all of our lives – delivered by the local coal man. I also recall my first home in Rose Street West, Old Penshaw, and how different life was for young housewives in those days. There were no luxuries like automatic washing machines, tumbledryers or dish washers then and all the household chores were done by hard work and effort.

However, it was not all about work in the two villages and there are many photographs of people enjoying themselves – sport, the cinema, amateur dramatics or just walking around the countryside that surrounds us.

The early history of the area is also remembered with stories about the famous Penshaw Monument and the development of the two communities over the years.

So enjoy this tour of Penshaw and Shiney Row and remember the olden days that are very different from now.

Lena Cooper
2010

Front Street, Shiney Row. From a postcard sent in 1912.

Penshaw Village. From a coloured postcard sent to 'Shiney Row, Bedlington' in 1926.

An unusual view of Old Penshaw Village. This was a postcard sent in 1911 and the stamp is postmarked 'Old Penshaw, Fence Houses.'

Acknowledgements

The author would like to thank the following who have helped with the publication of this book

For help with photographs:

Alan Brett, Ian S. Carr, Alan & Sheila Charlton, Andrew Clark, Harry Clark, Harry & Betty Ferry, Peter Gibson, Ellen Guthrie, Mary Hagley, Tom Hardy, Gloria Knowles, John Mawston, George Nairn, Peggy Ramshaw, John & Kenneth Stark, Denis & Freda Strafford, Ron Wilson, Shiney Row Male Voice Choir
Beamish – The North of England Open Air Museum

Special thanks to Shirley Shields for her help.

Sharyn Taylor for typing the manuscript for this book and for proof reading.

Bibliography

Sunderland 'Til I Die, Alan Brett & Andrew Clark
Mining Memories, Andrew Clark
Durham Coal – A People's History, Andrew Clark & George Nairn
Bridges of the River Wear, Keith Cockerill
Penshaw – The History of A Village, Dawn Cummings
Penshaw, Shiney Row, Philadelphia & Newbottle, Lena Cooper
Sunderland – A Century of Shopping, Philip Curtis
Wearside In Winter, Philip Curtis
The Story of The Villages – Bernard Gilpen Group, W.A. Curry, Shiney Row WI
Women of Old County Durham, Margaret McReady
Around Washington, Stuart Miller & George Nairn
Houghton-le-Spring and Hetton-le-Hole in Old Photographs, Ken Richardson
Shiney Row Remembered, Shiney Row Local History Society

Monthly Chronicles
Sunderland Echo

Poss Tubs and the Coal Man

I start this trip down memory lane of Penshaw and Shiney Row with some stories of how we used to live in the 1930s and '40s:

All the women in the colliery houses had a weekly agenda. Monday was always washing day. 'Possing' was not easy. It was hard just to lift the 'poss stick' let alone hit the clothes with any downward pressure. The scullery in my house in Penshaw had a post tub. If you were lucky you had a ringer with the tub. I would peg out the clothes in our backyard on the clothes line. Well at that time it was very hard work. It's like another world today where the young housewives have their automatic washing machines and tumbledryers. At least we had a long yard so I could get everything pegged out on the line. It was good because it meant everything would get dry at the same time.

Lena Cooper in 1945.

Tuesdays and Wednesdays were for ironing and putting clean clothes away, then the bedrooms had to be cleaned.

Thursday was baking day – with pies, teacakes, bread, scones, sponge cakes, custard tarts, and sometimes jam tarts and small queen cakes. All day was used for baking the food for the family to last for about a week.

Friday was always cleaning downstairs of the house from front door to back yard and occasionally after lunch there was some shopping to be done.

Saturdays were sometimes used for shopping in Sunderland or Newcastle according to how much spare cash was available for items required. This did not happen every week – just once in a while.

A kitchen in a Durham pit cottage. In the right hand corner is a washtub.

The Sabbath Day was kept holy – I went to a local chapel (long since converted into a dwelling house) in the morning. We went to Sunday school after dinner, then back to chapel again in the evening. This routine lasted until I was 13 when I was confirmed at St Barnabas Church, Burnmoor and began the same routine at the church.

The worst job – in those pre-war days – was cleaning the 'pit-clothes'. These were worn by male members of the family who worked down the local mines. Each item of clothing was full of coaldust and had to be 'dadded' against the wall in the back street to get rid of this. Then with an old knife the pit boots had to be freed from all the 'clarts' and rubbish that had built up on the sides and bottom of the boots, then greased.

I never understood why it was always my job to do this, just as it was always my job to scrub the scullery (kitchen) and pantry floors on a washing day after I got home from my job at the Co-op drapery department.

In the villages of Penshaw and Shiney Row a lot of men were employed at the local collieries. Herrington Colliery wasn't very far away and the men would make their way down the Maiden's Walk, across two fields and then to the pit. There were quite a number of other local pits like Whitefield – also known as Penshaw 'D' Pit. Most of the men had no choice but to go down the pit. What else was there to do when they left school? My brother Tom went down the pit but he had an accident when he had only been there a very short time. It caused him a lot of trouble and he wouldn't go back – he was frightened. He was only 16 years old and it had been his first job. So rather than go back down the pit he went down south and got a job in a hotel as a porter. He stayed in the south, got married and he worked his way up in the hotel business.

Two pit lads from Shiney Row or Newbottle. Reuben Peacock is on left. They are standing in the typical pose of the pitman – thumbs in their belts and carrying their safety lamps. Did these lads spend a lifetime in the pits like many thousands of men did in the mines in County Durham.

Two young 'uns putting the coals in. Miner's coal was often dumped onto the street for the younger members of the family to shovel it into the coal house.

Nearly all the men got coal delivered as part of their wages. As my husband wasn't a pitman we had to pay for our coal – remember these were the days when everyone used coal in their homes. We got our coal from Billy Carter who lived at Penshaw. He did a round and called at all of his customers. He would tip the bags you ordered into your coal house through a little door. Some weeks we couldn't afford coal and we would ask him not to call at ours – money was tight for my husband and me after the war.

Penshaw Monument

The foundation stone of the monument that adorns the hill around which the Lambton Worm is traditionally said to have coiled itself, was laid Wednesday August 28th 1844, by Thomas, Earl of Zetland Master of Free and Accepted Masons of England. The monument was erected to the memory of John George Lambton, Earl of Durham, who died at Cowes on 28th of July 1840, for "the distinguished services he rendered to his country, as an honest, able and patriotic statesman, and as the enlightened and liberal friend to the improvement of the people in morals, education, and scientific acquirements." Pensher Hill was chosen as the site, owing to its having been for many years connected with the property of the Lambton Family. It was estimated at the time that no fewer than 30,000 persons congregated at Pensher to witness the ceremony of the laying the foundation stone. The following inscription, which was placed on the lower stone, was tastefully engraved on a brass plate:-

This stone was laid by
THOMAS, EARL of ZETLAND
Grand Master of the Free and Accepted Masons of England assisted by
The Brethren of the Provinces of Durham and Northumberland on the 28th August 1844,
Being the Foundation Stone of a Memorial to be erected to the memory of
JOHN GEORGE, EARL OF DURHAM,
who, after representing the County of Durham in Parliament for fifteen years
Was raised to the Peerage and subsequently held the offices of Lord Privy Seal,
Ambassador Extraordinary and Minister at the Court of St. Petersburgh, and
Governor – General of Canada.
He died on 28th of July 1840, in the 49th year of his age.
The Monument will be erected
By the private subscriptions of the fellow countrymen,
Admirers of his distinguished talents and Exemplary private Virtues.
John and Benjamin Green Architects.

The design of the monument is copied from the Temple of Theseus. The dimensions, however, are exactly double those of the original. Thus, the columns of the Temple of Theseus are 3ft, 3in in diameter, while those of the Durham Memorial are 6ft, 6in. The total length of the structure is 100 ft, the width 53 ft, and the height from the ground 70 ft, at one end and 62 ft at the other. There are eighteen columns four at each end, and seven at the flanks or sides, counting two of the end ones on each flank. The monument occupies so commanding and conspicuous a position that it can be seen from almost all parts of the district between the lower reaches of the Tyne and Wear.

This article is taken from the *Monthly Chronicles* from its series 'North-Country Lore and Legend', September 1888. The article refers to the Lambton Worm wrapping itself around Penshaw Hill while many believe the story that it should be Worm Hill (see page 72). One of the old spellings of Penshaw is used – 'Pensher'.

Our Landmark

I could see Penshaw Monument from the next street where we lived. For the village of Penshaw, the Monument is our trademark or local landmark. I used to go to the Monument when they would have rolling the Easter eggs down the hill. The kids would have an outing to Penshaw Monument, perhaps with a picnic and some of kids made sledges to slide down the hill.

One of the pillars has steps inside and at one time you could climb to the top. What a wonderful view you must have had from the top of the Monument. Then a young lad fell and was killed and they closed the stairs for safety reasons.

Right: Rebuilding work on Penshaw Monument in the late 1970s. The photograph shows some of the stones down on the ground. They were carefully numbered so they could be returned to their right place. This much-loved landmark can be seen for miles around and the area is still a popular spot for visitors.

The Lambton Worm

Here are the opening lines, chorus and a verse on Penshaw Hill from this famous song :

One Sunday mornin' Lambton went
A-fishing in the Wear;
An' catched a fish upon he's heuk
He thowt leuk't vary queer.
But whatt'n a kind ov fish it was
Young Lambton cudden't tell
He waddn't fash te carry'd hyem,
So he hoyed it doon a well

Whisht lads, haad yor gobs
An' Aa'll tell ye aall an aaful story
Whisht lads, haad yor gobs
An' Aa'll tell ye 'boot the worm

This feorful worm would often feed
On caalves an' lambs an' sheep
An' swally little bairns alive
When they laid down te sleep
An' when he'd eaten aal he cud
An' he had had he's fill
He craaled away an' lapped he's tail
Ten times roond Pensha Hill.

Penshaw Then & Now

A view of Penshaw Monument with boy and dog playing on a haystack in the foreground around 1930.

Old Postcards

Here is a stamp postmarked 'Old Penshaw Fence Houses'. It is from the back of a postcard sent from Penshaw in 1911. Many of the views of Penshaw and Shiney Row in this book are taken from old picture postcards.

Today, we may only send a postcard while we are on holiday, however, for many years sending one from where you lived was common. So postcards were produced of local streets, buildings, people and events. A number of photographers toured the North East taking views of everyday life. These postcards have now become a valuable record of streets and buildings that are now long gone.

The golden age of the postcard was in the years before the First World War when hundreds of millions of cards were sent every year.

A wonderful view of Penshaw Village with a number of people posing for the photographer. In view are All Saints Church, the Grey Horse Inn, T&R Bird Cash Grocers and the Ship Inn.

This was a postcard sent to London in August 1912. The message reads: 'I shall be pleased to see you on Friday next at the Nelson Monument, Trafalgar Square at 7 pm. I leave Waterloo Station at 11.55 pm same night.'

The view from 2010 shows the shop between the two pubs has gone and the Ship Inn now re-named The Monument.

A postcard titled 'Penshaw Lane'. This postcard was sent in 1944 but the view is probably from an earlier date. Penshaw Monument is to the right in the background.

The same view in 2010. This main road from Chester-le-Street to Sunderland is now very busy. The postcard above seems to be a very rural scene in comparison.

Penshaw Lane on the corner of Chester Road around 1914. While most in the photograph are looking at the camera one man is seeing what is in the window of J.E. Thompson's grocery shop.

In 2010 J.E. Thompson's shop, like many in the village, has gone and has been converted into a house.

Penshaw Village after the Second World War. It shows a peaceful scene with the Ship Inn pub on the far left and the Monument on the right. A young lad sits on the pavement in front of the pub.

In 2010 the scene remains almost the same except the Ship Inn is now renamed The Monument.

Hill Farm House around 1913. Alice Ferry is holding Bill Humphrey at the door while Bill's mother looks through the window. The Ferry family came to Penshaw in 1898 to work on the farm.

The three Humphrey boys – Tom, Bill and Jack – at Hill Farm House before the First World War. The Humphreys had farmed in Penshaw for many years.

Gladstone Terrace in the 1920s. Is that the photographer's car in front of J. Elliott's draper shop. Some postcard photographers were know for including their cars in their pictures.

Gladstone Terrace from a postcard sent in 1936. The shop has now been taken over by J. Warnes. There are adverts for newspapers and cigarettes outside but on closer inspection it looks like hats are for sale in the left hand side of the window. Again only one car in the street.

Gladstone Terrace in 2010. This time it *is* the photographer's car in the foreground. While this picture was being taken a lady from one of these houses spoke to the photographer and was very pleased to hear about this book. She was very proud to be born and bred in Penshaw.

The postcard above, from the early 1900s, is titled 'Rainton Terrace, Old Penshaw'. The youngsters are wearing 'knickerbockers' that fastened at the knee and worn with long stockings. Short trousers came later. The woman on the right is wearing a long dress to her ankles – ladies would never show their knees or lower legs.

The same view in 2010 – now called Rainton Street.

The opening Ceremony of 1,000th house to be completed by Houghton-le-Spring Urban District Council on Wensleydale Avenue, Penshaw, on 11th August 1949. This was a time when thousands of houses were built by councils as part of the rebuilding programme after the Second World War.

Wensleydale Avenue in 2010 – still providing homes to local people over 60 years after being built.

The Prospect Inn, Penshaw in the years between the two world wars.

The pub in 2010 – now called the Country Park Inn.

Memories of Rose Street

My first home, not including living with my family and in laws, was in Rose Street, Penshaw in the 1940s. Here are my memories of our home – Number 10, Rose Street West:

After the war we lived in with Norman's mother in Garden Place till we could get a house. We lived at Number 23 and next door to us was the local policeman – PC McManus.

There was a man called George Reed who was involved with the business of letting houses. He used to collect the rent for these houses and used to call at Norman's mother house for hers. He got to know us through these visits and he knew we were looking for a house – he very kind and said he would do what he could for us.

Rose Street, Old Penshaw. The shop on the right appears to sell sweets with adverts for chocolates and pastilles. Over the years these shop had a few owners who tried selling different goods. One I remember tried selling jumpers and other clothes. Below is the same view in 2010. The shop has now been converted into a house.

Mr Reed got us a house in Rose Street West – number 10 – it had no upstairs. You came in the front door and through a tiny vestibule into the bedroom, which was also the front room. It had a living room come dining room come sitting room all in one. Then you had to go down two stone steps to a stone floor which was the scullery – that is what they were called then.

On the right side of the steps was a bench where you could do your washing and scrubbing or whatever. In the left hand corner was the pot boiler and at the very back of the scullery was the pantry. On the left side was the backdoor. The oven was in the front room and was heated by the coal fire.

Out the back was a long yard and part of it was made into a garden. Somebody who had lived in the house previously had made a garden about half the width of the yard. It was very useful for growing vegetables. On the other side of the yard was the wall connecting next door's house. Right at the bottom of the yard was the back gate and alongside the gate was the coal house. Next to the coalhouse was the lavatory. In those days the toilet had a wooden square top with a hole in the middle. It was an ash midden type toilet where the ashes from the fire were tipped into there to cover the 'deposits'.

These middens were emptied every so often by men with long handled shovels who came round and emptied the ashes and everything else into their carts to dispose of somewhere else. At that time there were few modern toilets like we know today. Inside toilets are a big improvement on what we had to use.

Rose Street, Old Penshaw. A postcard sent in 1914. The shop is named Bell's and appears to say: 'Meat Market – family butcher. There are also adverts for Lyon's Tea and Fry's Pure Cocoa. I believe at one point there was a fish and chip shop in the street.

Rose Street in 2010. Bell's shop on the right has been converted into a house like many former local shops. However, the shop on the left is still open and is now called Penshaw Aquatics and Pet Supplies. For many years this shop was a Post Office.

Memories of Shiney Row

C.A. Smith writing in the Sunderland Echo in 1962 wrote the following article called:

'Allens were a Shining Example to the People of Shiney Row'

The story of Shiney Row is illuminated by the lives of three people William, Charles and Elizabeth (better known as Betty) Allen. William was born in 1750, Charles in 1752, and both were sent down the pit at the age of seven, there to toil with other children for 18 hours a day for 3s a week!

As they seldom saw the light of day except in summer time they used to gather at the bottom of the shaft whenever they had a chance to gaze up as though through a telescope in reverse at the dim circle of light many fathoms above them where occasionally the sunlight filtered through the pall of dust and curling smoke. Girls and women found employment in the mines as their labour was cheap and Betty, who married William Allen in 1773, had helped her youthful companions to haul the tubs or corves along the low tunnelled ways.

Bent Double

Such haulage was performed by chains attached to leather belts round their waists, and for long periods women workers had to proceed almost bent double so they resembled: it is said "a line of walking triangles." Fortunately, Betty was able to give up this arduous employment before she suffered the permanent disfigurement of curvature of the spine which was the lot of many. Wages were low – the top wage of 12s a week being paid to hewers so that the sum of 3s earned by the children added up to a very useful total if the family was a large one. The dangers were manifold for miners worked by naked candle light and thus explosions were of frequent occurrence. It was at Fatfield I believe, that the first official report of a colliery explosion was made in this area. On August 18, 1708 a violent conflagration burst up from the pit mouth "like the firing of a cannon" and 68 lives were lost. In fact so great was the force that two men and one woman were blown up from the shaft bottom, 57 fathoms in depth, high up into the air. This disaster called immediate attention to a need for proper systems of ventilation and for a safety lamp which would not ignite sulphur and dust in places which lacked a free passage of air.

Front Street, Shiney Row, around 1910.

Lighted Candles

We can well understand why Betty was so anxious to save her husband from such risks, especially as it was years before any real progress resulted in the mitigation of such deplorable conditions below. At the bottom of the pit the Allens and their workmates replete with tools, candles and matches used to wait until the deputy viewer told them "She's safe" and then proceeded along the main way with their lighted candles stuck in lumps of clay held in the palms of their hands. Often they were pushed along lying face upwards in a "rolley" by young boys who crawled along the low wagon ways. These were days, too when miners descended by the "loop" method and in distain left the chain and safer basket corf to the young employees. For all their efforts the Allens had no money to spare because they provided not only for themselves but for other branches of their family who had been left almost destitute by thriftless parents. Indeed both William and Betty had been brought up without regard for religion and so they lived for several years after their marriage. Their first home was at Pelaw, and then in succession at Philadelphia, Penshaw and Shiney Row. Betty is described as a neat, sensible and industrious young woman with dark hair and clear, penetrating eyes, good features and a fine blush of health in her cheeks. In figure she was straight and well proportioned and in character and choice of apparel not without severity. We can picture her wearing a grey or black dress without any trinkets or ornaments a neatly crimped cap and out of doors a "scuttle" bonnet with a shawl pinned across her shoulders – all in the prevailing Quaker style. She believed that beauty in dress consisted i not being conspicuous and not over loading the human form with unnatural devices or additions. One thinks of Horace's " Simplex Munditiis," but Betty, though "plain and neatness" was no Pyrrha – indeed it is said that she seldom smiled and never laughed.

Shiney Row United Methodist Free Church around 1900.

Rarely Smiled

Blessed as she was with common sense, honour, industry, integrity, thrift and tenderness. She seems to have been the undisputed head of the household. William Allen is described as short and round of form and with a pug nose though his features were regular his eyes grey and like Betty, he rarely smiled: yet his gravity was less marked than hers. He was a man of few words, possessed of a kindly disposition, fond of peace and so seldom ruffled or upset by difficulties. Without Betty he would probably have passed into oblivion unrecorded.

Conversion of the Allens occurred after Betty had been invited by a friend to attend an evening service at Houghton-le-Spring Parish Church, where the Rev John Rotherham was famed for his preaching and liked by people of all denominations. The confession and the prayers revealed to Betty her spiritual needs and she induced William as well as Charles, who resided with them, to become staunch adherents of the faith. By their example it was not long before cottage meetings were held to which Wesleyan preachers expounded the word to those whose tears of repentance streamed down their work-begrimed faces. Such enthusiasm was bound to spread, and it was not long before a permanent chapel was required.

In Business

We saw how anxious Betty was for William and Charles to leave the pits – now there was further incentive to raise money for the chapel. In Penshaw Betty opened a grocer's shop which twice failed owing to her lack of experience and education. But Betty would not hear of defeat. They moved to Shiney Row and again she went into business which this time succeeded. William served at the counter while Charles delivered the orders with the aid of a donkey called after himself – a rare instance of Betty's humour!

Allen House is still in existence as a bakery and catering establishment. It passed to Mr Hedworth Banks, well known for his support of "Banks Chapel," who carried on his butchering business in the former Allen premises. It belongs now to Yates family. Before the Allens left Penshaw they had contributed a little money and much service to the building of a Wesleyan Chapel opened in 1783 which catered for Shiney Row, Penshaw, Cox Green etc. It was William Allen who in 1778 obtained possession of the site – a piece of land on the village green from Edward Lazenby – probably the very spot where John Wesley had preached in 1751. With the help of other Methodists, subscriptions to cover the cost were obtained and the chapel was erected by its well-wishers who hewed the stone from Penshaw Quarry.

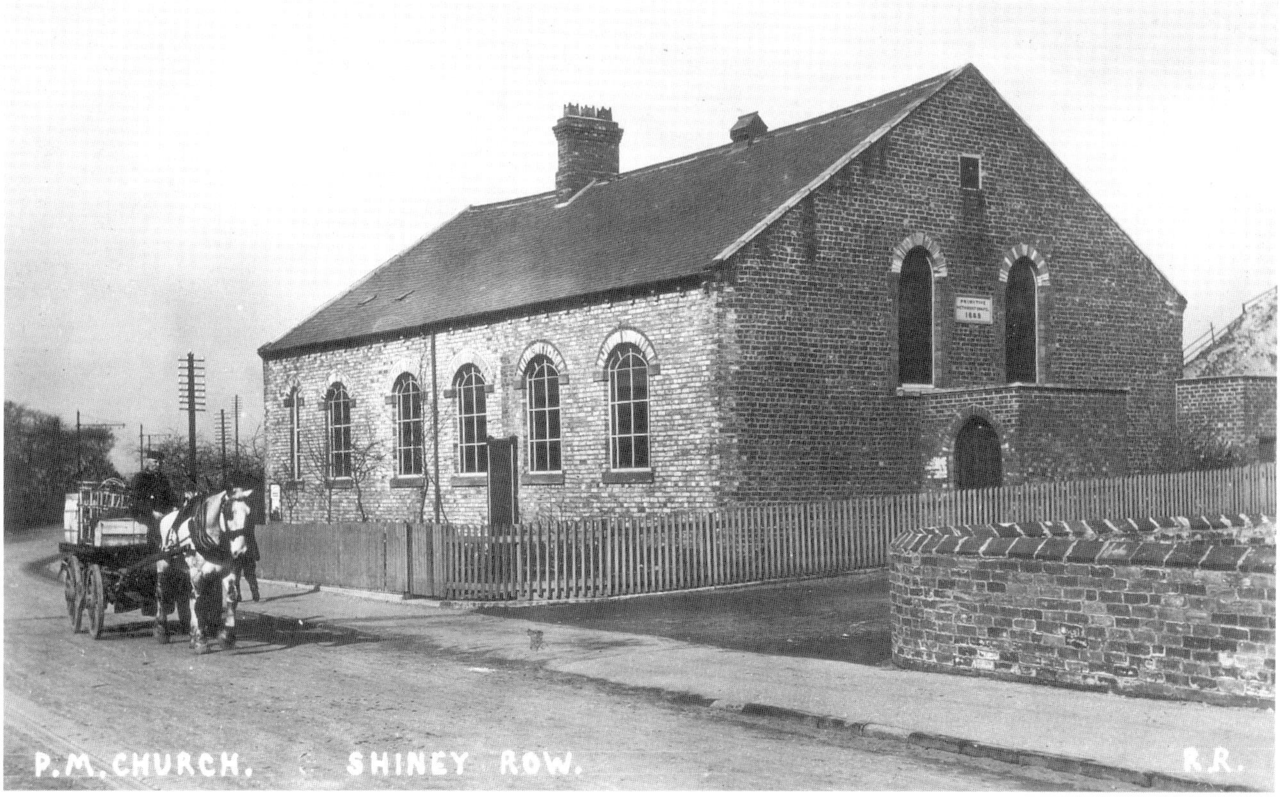

Primitive Methodist Church, Shiney Row, around 1902. The date on the side of the building looks like 1868.

£100 From Family

So the Allens became prominent in the Old Penshaw Society. On their removal to Shiney Row their business continued to prosper and in 1805 Betty's dream came true when the new chapel was opened. William, as before, obtained the land and collected the subscriptions, including £100 from his own family. Sir Henry Vane Tempest, father of the Marquess of Londonderry, who owned this piece of land, subscribed £150 thanks to the forthrightness of William Allen. It would take too long to tell the whole of this fascinating story, but as their business flourished so the Allens contributed a goodly portion of their income to the Chapel and other charitable organisations. Mr John Ward, of Ward and Story, Solicitors of Durham was their legal advisor and staunch adherent as was Mr Michael Longridge of Hunters Hall, Sunderland. The Chapel was afterwards used by the United Methodists as well, and again required enlargement. William Allen died in 1823 at the age of 73, Charles died in 1832 aged 80, and Betty ended her life of loyalty and service a few years later. In 1830 the Shiney Row Chapel was enlarged and Billy Dawson the special preacher for the occasion, with great dramatic power, pictures heaven coming down to Shiney Row and Shiney Row taken up to heaven in the persons of William and Betty Allen.

St Oswald's Church, Shiney Row.

Methodism sprang out of the darkness of the Industrial Revolution as a shining beacon light which comforted and illuminated the lives and homes of the poor and downtrodden with new hope, new purpose, and new faith. Loving hands hewed the stone from the local quarry to build the chapels, vice was stamped out for many lives, a new respect for themselves and faith in God succeeded.

So it was at Shiney Row which through the devoted service of the Allens an their fellows became a "Shining example" to all.

Of course the Allens prospered as they deserved and as they had freely received so they "freely gave." Clear vision and sound judgement ensured that their benefactions were wisely bestowed and today the benefit of their faithful service and generosity still abides.

The War Memorial in Shiney Row – remembering those who lost their lives from the Parish of Penshaw during the First World War.

Shiney Row Then & Now

Front Street, Shiney Row in the 1920s. On the right is Westbourne Terrace – a mixture of shops, businesses and houses. The Swan Inn public house is on the right.

The same view of Shiney Row in 2010. Now all of Westbourne Terrace has been converted into shops and other businesses – the houses have gone. The Swan Inn and the buildings behind were demolished a number of years ago.

Shiney Row looking towards Herrington Burn. A postcard sent to Norwich in 1915. The message on the back includes: 'Do you know this view – it is not very clear but you will be able to make it out.'

A much clearer view of the road down to Herrington Burn in 2010. This is now a busy route through the area and not the quiet street with no traffic as above.

Quarry Row, Shiney Row in the 1920s. On the left you can just glimpse the Walter Willson grocery store. Behind the group of people is Penshaw Place and the Wesleyan Chapel can be seen on the left.

The Shoulder of Mutton public house is the main building remaining in 2010.

Right: Barrack Row, Shiney Row, before the Second World War.

Perhaps that is a pitman walking along. In those days there would be no pithead baths and the men would come home covered in coal dust. At home, out would come the tin bath that hung in the backyard on a nail. The bath would be filled with hot water in front of the fire. That's how the men washed but they were used to it. Pit baths came later and it was a real luxury for the men who could come home in the same condition they left – clean!

Barrack Row in 2010. How many pitmen have lived in this street over the years?

A Message For You

Here is a stamp postmarked 'Shiney Row' from an old picture postcard. Today if want to communicate with someone we can use the phone, text or email and they will have our message in no time at all. One hundred years ago the nearest equivalent was the postcard. Some of the postcards used in this book have simple messages on the back. Such as 'hope you are well' or 'I will be seeing you soon.' It was common to send to a friend or relative who lived nearby a postcard on a morning and they would receive it in the afternoon. This was when there was more than one delivery a day.

The United Methodist Church in the 1920s. It was built in 1805 and enlarged in 1830.

In 2010 this site is the home of the Trinity Methodist Church.

Sporting Life

Members of Shiney Row Star Football Club in the 1920s.

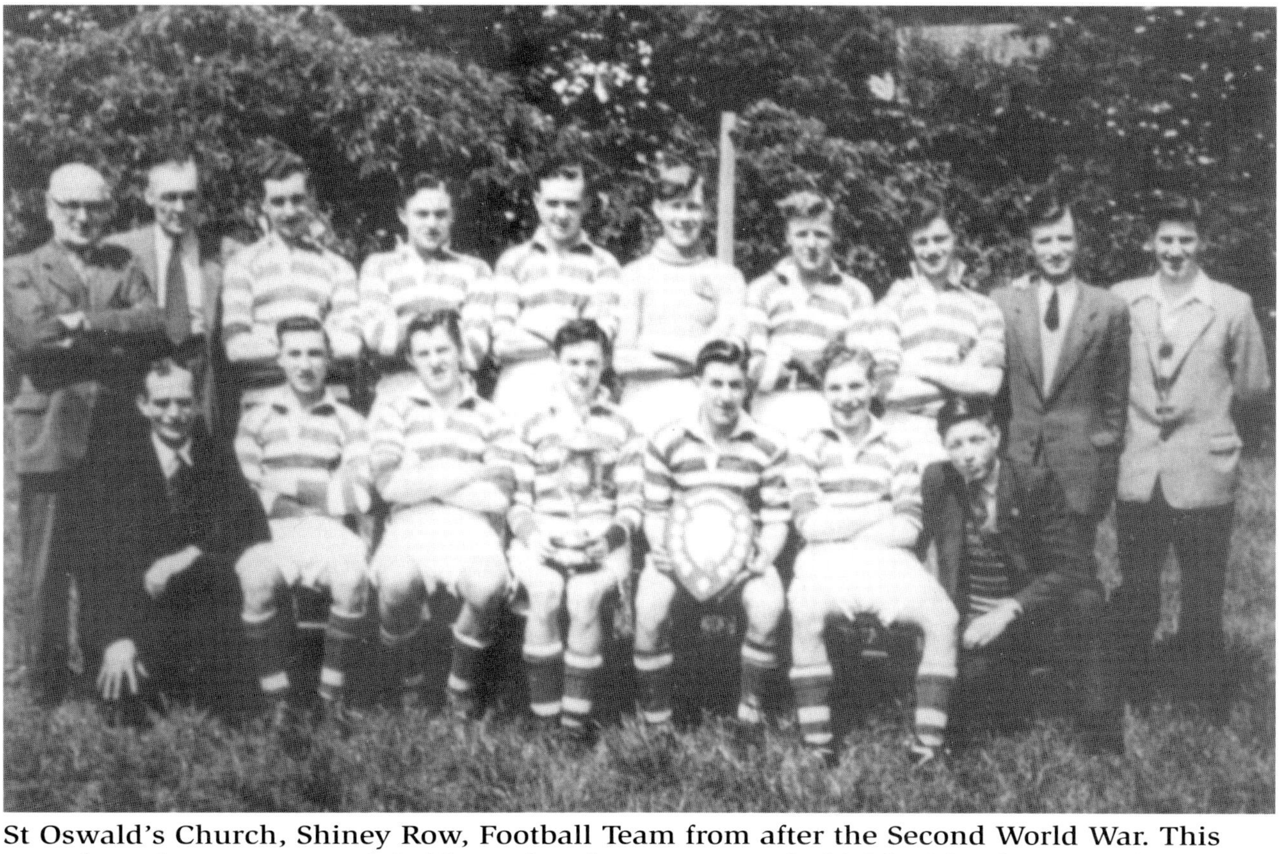

St Oswald's Church, Shiney Row, Football Team from after the Second World War. This must have been a successful side as they have a cup and shield – like the team above.

Shiney Row Junior School football team, 1962-63. Back row: J. Lister, Ken Harland, Alex Scorer, B. Ramshaw, D. Scott, S. Lynn, D. Howe, unknown, Mr Lister. Middle row: B. Poulter, D. Horton, J. Metcalf, K. Kennedy, T. Cornish, J. Pugh, L. Carter. Front row: Tommy ?, Alan Kennedy, G. Calvert, Peter Robinson. The team were the winners of the Joseph Cup in 1962-63. Alan Kennedy later played professional football for Newcastle, Liverpool and Sunderland. He also represented England.

Alan Kennedy

Alan Kennedy had a very successful football career. As a teenager he broke into the Newcastle United team and played in the 1974 FA Cup Final against Liverpool. The Merseyside club then paid £330,000 for the services of the young full back in 1978. Seven years and over 250 League appearances later, he signed for Sunderland for a £100,000 fee.

The highlight of his career came in 1981 when he scored the winning goal for Liverpool in the European Cup Final against Real Madrid. Alan played for England when Bobby Robson chose him for an international against Northern Ireland in April 1984. He won a second England cap the following month against Wales.

After retiring from playing, Alan has become an 'after-dinner speaker'. His agent's website describes Alan as:

'From Shiney Row to European Glory'.

Right: Alan in his Liverpool days.

A Penshaw Church football team from the 1921-22 season. Sitting in the middle is the minister – John Taylor. Below him is a young mascot holding the ball.

Another Penshaw Church football team this time from the 1922-23 season. This team has two trainers – the ones with the towels over their shoulders.

Above: L. Taylor and friends playing cricket with South Terrace, Shiney Row in the background.

Left: New Penshaw Netball team, 1952. Back row: Teacher, Miss E. Cooper, Margaret Preston, Gloria Jefferson, Lorna Dobson, Maureen Winwood. Front row: Ruth Nelson, Mary Gould, Joyce Howe, Margaret Thompson.

Right: Penshaw Salvation Army Keep Fit Team, at the Penshaw Hall. Left to right: Eva Nelmes, Freda Jenkins, Sheila Jenkins, Jean Gould, Mary Jefferson, Gloria Jefferson, Joyce Howe, Ann Gould, Mary Gould, Margaret Barker, Pearl White, Laura Dinsdale, Margaret Mould, Jenny Henderson.

Penshaw Community Association Carpet Bowls team in the early 1970s. A successful team with cups and medals. Left to right: Alan Smith, Diane Faith, Alan Charlton, Hughie Jackson, Harry Ferry, Gordon Chapman, Jean Chapman, George Lumsden, Ellen Faith, Harry Ferry Jnr, Herbie Binns and George Marsden.

Penshaw Community Association Carpet Bowls team in the early 1980s. Back row: Page Hargrave, Harry Ferry, Peter Shale, Alf Richardson and George Marsden. Front row: Frank Mole, Margaret Mole, Ellen Faith and George Lumsden. The team is still going strong today.

Working Life

During the Second World War I trained to be a nurse at Preston Hospital in North Shields. However, I had to leave nursing because of an injury to my elbow made it very difficult for me to help lift the patients. I had broken a bone in my elbow when I fell when I was a child. It was winter and we were sliding on the ice in the school playground – I fell and broke a bone.

After the war I was out of work until somebody said one of our neighbours needed some help. After helping there I was asked to look after a nice young couple – Betty and Ray. Betty was pregnant and she asked, "Lena, will you look after me when I have the baby?"

I said, "Yes, of course I will. You needn't worry about it – I am there for you."

She and her husband Ray used to go to her mother's at Fatfield on a Sunday where they would have their dinner. This particular Sunday at her mother's she started having the baby. So consequently her mother got the job of looking after her. Betty had to stay there and in those days you were allowed to stay in bed a fortnight. It did mean I was out of a job.

There was a District Nurse called Nurse Forster and she got to knew me through Betty – she used to visit her and the baby to check everything was ok. She was a nice person and Betty of course had told her what the arrangement was when she had the baby. Nurse Forster must have kept me in mind because I got a visit from her and she said would I go and look after another young couple where the women had just had her baby – a little boy. I got the job for two weeks of looking after her.

Lena when she was a nurse during the Second World War.

I was approaching the second week and I never saw any sign of any wages. I thought maybe I was supposed to do this for free. We needed the money because neither me or my husband were working. Anyhow, I thought well I have to try and get a job where I would get paid. However, I got another visit from Nurse Forster and she said I have another job for you Lena. I said, "Well, I hope this one pays." She didn't know I hadn't been getting paid but she quickly made sure I was. Apparently the young couple hadn't sent the form in that they were supposed to send in to agree to this payment. So I got paid eventually.

The next job Nurse Forster gave me was to look after a man who was almost blind who lived with his wife who had cancer and his son who had TB. So I looked after them. I did everything – washing, scrubbing of floors, baking – you name it I was doing. Sometimes I think I was more round their house than I was at my own house because there seemed to be much more to be done there. The wife died not long after I started. Their son, Billy, had just come back from the Sanatorium with TB. He eventually got a job on the buses as a conductor. He was a lovely lad – very nice natured as the father was too.

Although I enjoyed the work, the wages I was getting weren't really sufficient because my husband still hadn't got a job. The hours were also very long. I had been looking after this family for two years when a next door neighbour offered to come in and help so I took the opportunity to look for another job. I saw a copy of the evening paper and in it Binns were advertising for staff in the office. At that time Binns were one of the big department stores in Sunderland. I applied thinking I wouldn't get it – I applied and just took pot luck. I was lucky and I got the job.

I worked at Binns for several years before applying for a job at the Coal Board.

Binns Department Store in Fawcett Street, Sunderland, after the Second World War. The Town Hall with its familiar clock is in the middle of the photograph. Binns closed in 1992.

Working For The Coal Board

I started working for the National Coal Board in 1955, in the Mechanisation Department. My immediate 'Boss' was George Renwick who was in charge of the mechanisation of the local mines. Machinery was taking over a lot of the hard back-breaking work of the miners. A mining revolution! He had a team of men to help organise and get this system working.

Then one morning the Senior Clerical Officer showed me an internal staff circular he had just received, asking for applications for a clerical vacancy in the Chairman's Office. After a lot of persuasion and careful thought, I finally applied for the vacancy. It was one of the best decisions I ever made. I was granted an interview and, when that special day arrived, I was almost a nervous wreck. But I got the job.

A short time after I started in the Chairman's office, the new Chairman, Dr William Reid took over. When we moved to Team Valley Trading Estate offices, there were three of us who were Chairman's staff, his secretary, a typist and myself.

Three of the many VIPs who visited Dr Reid were: Lord Robens – Chairman of the National Coal Board from 1961 to 1971, a strong character at the time. Dr Bronowski – the intellectual thinker, a quiet-voiced man, gentle mannered. Sam Watson – of the National Union of Mineworkers, Durham Area, a pleasant 'man of the people'.

Chairman of the NCB's Durham Division, Sir William Reid, with, right to left, his secretary, Muriel Melville, confidential clerk, Lena Cooper, and typist, Lilian Richardson.

Transport

A train passes by Cox Green Station signal box. This station closed to passenger traffic in 1964 but continued for some time for goods.

Penshaw Station looking towards Cox Green in 1924. Note the sign for OXO. The station is very neat and tidy and shows the great pride that was taken in the appearance of local stations.

Above: A scavenger cart in Shiney Row between the two world wars. The driver is Alf Day. At this time horse and carts were a common sight in local streets. In those days most deliveries were by horse and cart, such as from the Co-op Stores.

Right: A telegram boy with his bicycle in the Shiney Row area, around 1910.

Before the age when telephones were common sending a telegram was the quickest form of communication for urgent messages. A few years later boys such as this one would regularly be delivering telegrams informing families of the death of loved ones in the First World War.

Left: The tram crew beside Tram No 18 at Penshaw Station Banktop, 1913. The tram was bound for Houghton-le-Spring. The conductor, with his tickets and money bag slung over his shoulders, is on the left.

Transport

The trams were on their way out when I was young. Perhaps in our area they disappeared when I was in my teens before the Second World War. They were still around in other areas after the war. The trams were replaced by buses which weren't as posh as they were in later years. I remember buses that had wooden seats not leather ones!

I rarely used the trains when I lived at Penshaw. We lived in Old Penshaw but the station was at New Penshaw. If I got the train to Penshaw it was a very steep walk up the bank to home.

Below: Another scavenger cart in Shiney Row. The driver is Luke Wilson.

Mining

An engine pulling a train of coal wagons at Penshaw in the 1960s. Trains such as this filled with coal from local collieries would make the journey to Sunderland where colliers would take the fuel to the South of England or Europe.

C75 USE BLOCK LETTERS

SENDER DATE..........195....

NATIONAL COAL BOARD

Durham Division No. 2 Area

Penshaw

A/c of

TO HOWDON GAS WORKS

BRITISH RLYS..........SECN

VIA..........

Wagon Letter & Number		Weight T. C.
	1	

Description— W. Singles

Consignee— Northern Gas Board

HARLOW B4835

Date of Weighing : ....

Date of Despatch : ....

Seller and Place of Weighing :

N.C.B., Northumberland & Durham Division

No. 1 Area - PENSHAW COLLIERY

WASHED DOUBLES

WAGON NUMBER	SALE WEIGHT OF FUEL
TARE ....T..........C	..........T..........C

Date of Weighing : ....

Date of Despatch : ....

Seller and Place of Weighing :

N.C.B., Northumberland & Durham Division

No. 1 (D) Area - PENSHAW COLLIERY

1½" ROUGH SMALL

WAGON NUMBER	SALE WEIGHT OF FUEL
TARE ....T..........C	..........T..........C

Above: Three wagon labels from Penshaw which were put on railway trucks to indicate the weight, type of coal and destination. Washed doubles was the best coal and used overseas or shipped to London. Rough small was used in power stations.

Right: A wagon label from Herrington.

From Herrington Washer

WORKMEN'S GRADED COAL

No. DATE 196

TONS CWTS.

Above: Band with Lodge Officials and Banner from New Herrington Colliery in April 1953. The conductor of the band was G. Steele.

Left: A packed Durham City on the day of the Miners' Gala – or 'Big Meeting Day'. This celebration of mining traditions in County Durham was one of the highlights of the year for pitmen and their families. How many from Penshaw and Shiney Row looked forward to this day?

A view of New Herrington Colliery by Sunderland photographer Ian S. Carr. For fifty years Ian recorded the changing face of railways, mining and shipbuilding in the North East.

New Herrington Colliery during demolition with Penshaw Monument in the background. The pit closed in 1985 and the former mining site has been landscaped into a country park.

At Work

A group of teachers at Penshaw School after the First World War. Included are: Miss Hudson, Mr Laider, Mr Batey, Mr C. Oliver, Miss Carse, Miss M. George, Miss Todd, Mr J. Mole, Miss Sherriff, Miss Livesy, Miss I. Robertson, Miss Haslam, Miss M. Brody (later Mrs Smith), Miss M. Agar and Miss P. French.

More teachers at Penshaw School. Included are: Miss I. Robinson, Miss M. Boddy (later Mrs Smith), Miss N. Agar, Miss Sherriff, Miss Gordon, Miss E. Boddy (later Mrs Park).

A group of workers from Shiney Row Coke Works, around 1930.

A group of lady workers in the New Herrington/Shiney Row area. Does any reader recognise a relative?

Above: Alf Hind & Sons General Dealers and Hardware Merchants, Shiney Row, around 1930. A sign above the windows says: 'Decorators for over a century ... Painters, Glaziers, Paperhangers ... House, Church & Sign Decorators.'

Left: Mr Hind, the Builder, in his garden. Shiney Row Councillor John Mawston served his apprenticeship with this company, Alf Hind & Sons Builders, Decorators, General Dealers and Hardware Merchants.

The Shiney Row Branch of the Newbottle Co-operative Stores, around the 1920s. At the top of the building is the date 1905.

The former Co-op building in 2010. Like many former Co-ops it has had a number of tenants since it closed its doors. The building is now the home of Shiney Advice & Resource Project – ShARP – and the Shiney Diner.

Left: Harry Low's Barber's Shop, Coffin Row, Shiney Row, 1910. Standing in the doorway, wearing the bowler hat and waistcoat, is Mr Low. He is with his daughter Nina and his assistant Joe Combey – dressed very business-like with his apron, boots and flat cap. A barber's pole is hanging above the door while the shop window has a fine display of cigarettes, tobacco and pipes.

This shop was in Coffin Row, opposite Westbourne Terrace, and was so called because of its shape. Coffin Row was demolished alongside a number of the older streets in Shiney Row. It had a number of shops but not as many as the busier Westbourne Terrace.

Shopping

There used to be lots of small corner shops. At the end of my street in Penshaw, Rose Street West, was a grocery shop owned by Jack Faide. In the middle of the street was a fish shop and on Rose Street East, which was opposite Rose Street West, was a shop which had a very nice lady who was a confectioner. They were all busy shops because there was no supermarkets like today so we had to depend on the little local shop at the end of our streets.

On the main street in Penshaw was a bakery – Kate Johnson– Kate's we used to call it and they baked some really lovely home-made stuff. Her pies were lovely!. It wasn't all that expensive and must have been reasonably priced for people to go. It was cheaper than having to buy the stuff and bake your own.

If you wanted anything more substantial than the little shops could provide you would go to Shiney Row to do your shopping. I used to go down to a shop called the Red Stamp Store. At the Red Stamp Stores you got a book and every time you did your shopping you put some red stamps in this book. Then, when it was full, you could buy your next week's groceries and that sort of thing. However, this store wasn't there very long and Stewart's took over shop.

The best place to shop in the area was the Co-op at Shiney Row. There were two Co-ops. The branch of the Chester-le-Street Co-op on Boult Terrace and a Newbottle Co-operative Stores on the road down to Herrington Burn.

For any other shopping you could always go on the bus to Sunderland – if you could afford it. But how many people could afford to do that in those days? It wasn't a very lucky time for money as not everyone had a job.

Left: W. Inch's confectioner's shop in Shiney Row. Mrs Inch is standing between the two men on the doorstep. This was one of many local shops in the area in the days before supermarkets.

Rationing

We had rationing right up to the early 1950s. You would have thought rationing would have ended after the Second World but things came off ration very gradually over the years. But everyone coped with rationing – you had to get use to it. The war was on from 1939 to 1945 you know!

There were ways of getting around the shortages of food and other goods in the shops. What we would do was swap your rations. If you didn't like something you swapped with someone else who did. When rationing did end in the 1950s everyone seemed to go berserk. All of a sudden you could get what you wanted.

The Co-op

The two local Co-op Stores sold mainly groceries. If there was something you wanted and they didn't have it they could order it from their main store which would be Newbottle or Chester-le-Street. Although the branches didn't sell everything they were alright for weekly shopping where you buy the usual things each week. With every purchase you quoted your dividend number so you could build up your dividend that was paid out around every six months – it was a good way of saving money. When I was younger I would say my grandparent's number when I shopped at the Co-op but when I started working at the Co-op I got my own number. I can still remember my dividend number – 2044. My grandparents was 3399. It's amazing that I can still remember these numbers after all these years but if you ask most people they can still recall these four digits.

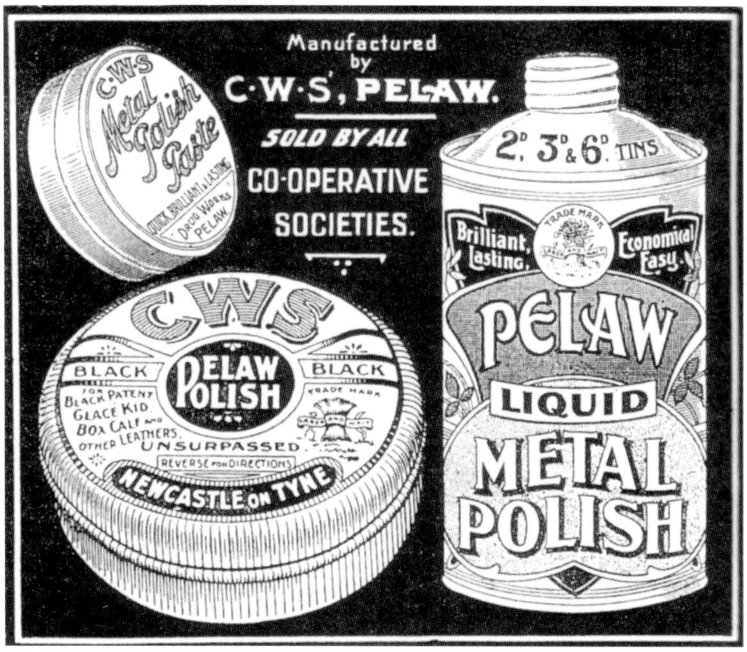

An advert for Co-op polish from the Chester-le-Street Co-operative's 'History and Handbook of the Arrangements in Connection with the Society's Jubilee' in 1912. It was manufactured at the Co-op's factory in Pelaw.

A close up view of the Shiney Row Branch of the Chester-le-Street Co-op Store on Boult Terrace. Above the windows are signs for Grocery and Butchering. In the upper windows are signs for Boots & Shoes and Drapery.

Working at the Co-op

In the 1930s the variety of jobs open to women where I lived was somewhat limited. There was the local brick factory (Lumley Brickworks) which employed women to deal with some of the brick-making processes. In 1935/36 I was told of a vacancy in the office of the Chester-le-Street Co-operative Society Bakery Department. Being advised to apply for the post, I did and got the job. At the time I had no idea what was involved in this. I discovered that my starting time was 6 am and the finishing could be approximately 3 or 4 pm.

My first morning I had to be out of bed at 5 am, dressed – breakfasted and on my way for my three mile walk to Chester-le-Street to start work at 6 am. At that time there were no service buses before 6 am – so I had to walk.

When I got to work, my first job was in the office, checking the bakery orders from the various Co-op Branches and taking orders by telephone. When all the orders were written up they were taken into the bakehouse for their attention and packing on to the bakery boards for the vans to do branch deliveries.

My next duty was to stay in the bakehouse and grease tins for that day's batch of pies, cakes etc. The bakehouse was on the first floor and below at the ground level was the tea-room. On odd occasions I was told to service the tea-room. That was where I learned how to make a pot of tea and how to toast a teacake.

After a while I was able to get transferred to Fence Houses Branch in the drapery department. The bakery was to be closed. Nothing to do with me – honest!

Here I am while I worked at Fence Houses Co-op in the 1930s. I'm sitting on the knee of Mr Hutchinson, the delivery driver. To the right is George Carr, centre is Harry Hamilton and on the left is Jimmy Green.

So it was much better in all ways – start at 9 am and just a short walk to work. I was about 17 years old and reckoned I only had to put in one year in this job then I could apply to become a nurse, which was what I wanted to be – but I had to be 18 before I could apply.

Working in the drapery department of the Co-op (Fence Houses Branch) was enjoyable up to a point but I hated having to do the chores at home that involved getting my nails dirty!

The Shiney Row Branch of the Chester-le-Street Co-op Store. This branch was on Boult Terrace. This postcard was send from Sunderland to Shiney Row in July 1907.

Boult Terrace in 2010. The Co-op has gone and now the building is the home of Shiney New Appliances – 'Factory Prices Direct To You!'

Public Houses

The Wheat Sheaf Inn, Shiney Row, with a large group of men outside in 1925. One young girl is standing at the front and a lone boy to the far left. The pub is still popular 85 years later.

Above: Harry Ramshaw, Harry Davison and Roy Parish in the Grey Horse pub, Penshaw.

Left: Outside the Ship Inn, Penshaw, around the time of the First World War. The landlord, Harry Watson, is on the far right. Note the two men in uniform. This old village pub is now named The Monument.

An old photograph of the Swan Inn, Shiney Row in 1930.

Two views of the Oddfellows Arms in Shiney Row. The main structure of the building has remained the same over the years although the 2010 view on the right shows the front of the building has been refurbished.

Local People

The people of Penshaw and Shiney Row have always been pleasant and helpful to me. Some of them suffered hard times but they didn't let that bother them.

They are good people.

Gloria (Jefferson) Knowles with daughter Sue and friend Valerie Truman in the gardens of The Poplars, Old Penshaw.

Florrie Chicken in the back garden of The Poplars, Old Penshaw. The Methodist Chapel is in the background.

A group of local people at Shiney Row: W.M. Robinson, Mr King, Mary Taylor, unknown, Mr Wordsley, Mrs Vardy, B. Stains, Mary Bissett, M. Taylor, Peggy Welsh.

Above: A wedding car believed to be in the Shiney Row area. The date is probably in the 1920s and at this time there would be very few cars seen in the street. Today, some married couples hire cars such as these to make their wedding day extra special.

Right: Workers at Hill Farm, Penshaw, in the years between the two world wars. Alf Ferry is believed to be the man at the back in the suit.

Right: Outside 26 Collingwood Drive, Shiney Row are: Myra Greenwell, Bell Hindmarsh and Freda Strafford.

Left: A flower show at Penshaw Community Hall in the late 1970s. Included in the photograph are: Alma Wilson, Mrs Wilson, George Lumsden, Betty Ferry and Lesley Ferry.

The opening of the Village in Bloom Trough in 1995. Included are: Betty & Harry Ferry, Maureen & John Curry, Jimmy McBeth and George Marsden.

A presentation for Penshaw Community Association Carpet Bowls in the 1970s. Left to right: Jenny Palmer, George Lumsden, Sid Jackson, Harry Ferry Jnr, George Marsden, Harry Ferry Snr, Ellen Faith, Alan Smith and Herbie Binns.

A group of local men in London for Sunderland's visit to Wembley for the League Cup Final in 1985. Left to right: Gordon Chapman, George Marsden, Frankie Mole, Dick Lane, Alan Charlton and Bob Simmonds. Bob later became leader of Sunderland Council.

John Mawston

John Mawston, from Shiney Row, has served local people for many years as a Councillor. Above are two photographs taken when he was Chairman of Houghton Urban District Council in 1967-68. On the left he is at Houghton Feast with Member of Parliament Tom Urwin.

On the photograph above right he is at the opening of a fayre at Penshaw Place Methodist Church, Shiney Row.

John joined Sunderland Council after the merger with Houghton. In 1987-88 he had the honour of becoming Mayor of Sunderland.

Left: Here is John during his time as Sunderland's Mayor with his aunt, Selena Parr, who was his Mayoress during his year in office.

Two photographs from Houghton Feast in 1967. *Above*: John Mawston blows the whistle to start a game of 'pushball'. *Below*: John turns the ox on the spit – a tradition of Houghton Feast.

Sad Times

When I married my husband Norman in 1941 I had to move down to Birmingham because that's where he was working in the Austin Factory. During the war you went where you were told to help in the effort to defeat Germany. We lived in furnished rooms all the war years. However, when I was pregnant and going to have my daughter, Maureen, I came back home and lived in with Norman's mother which in those days is what you did. You didn't go into hospital like nowadays. There was a local lady who was a midwife and she helped to guide me on the right track as I was just a young person. I was helped by a local nurse from one of the houses in the estate – she was the one that came to deliver my baby on 28th November 1942. Maureen was born in Norman's mother's house – No 23 Garden Place, Penshaw. After that I stayed in Penshaw – I didn't want to take the baby to Birmingham.

Garden Place, Penshaw.

One day Maureen developed a cold and as I had been a nurse I thought I could cope with this. But when she was vomiting a lot of phlegm, red lights flashed in my brain. I thought this was more than a cold. I called the doctor in who was visiting someone in our street and asked him to check Maureen out because I was worried. The doctor wasn't too happy to do that as he I had called him in off the street. He came in and he checked her. He then told me to wrap her up well, put a coat on and get in his car as we were going through to the hospital in Sunderland. Which was very good of him I suppose but he didn't have much option. Two days later Maureen died and it was the biggest blow of my life.

Maureen was buried in her grandfather's grave at Penshaw. My husband's father had a government grave because he had served in the First World War. I didn't want Maureen to be buried anywhere – she was my daughter and I wanted her to be respected even in death. I was very strong on that. Norman's mother made the suggestion and I make some inquires. We talked to the Bishop of Jarrow and put the situation to him to ask for permission. Permission was granted but there were some strict rules. She was buried in the right hand corner of the grave and we weren't allowed to put her name on the headstone. Also we weren't allowed to put flowers on the grave. These were the two rules because it was a government grave.

The interior of All Saints Church, Penshaw.

In 2010, I returned to the graveyard at Penshaw. The churchyard has changed a lot in the past 68 years and I couldn't find the headstone of my daughter's grave.

Stark's DIY

Denis Stark was my cousin. When my grandparents died his mam and dad came to live with us. So Denis grew up with me.

He set up his DIY business in the 1960s and it soon became a success. His two sons grew up and joined the business and eventually took over.

The gates of D. Stark Ltd – established in 1964.

Here, on the right, is my Aunt Lena – Denis Stark's mother. She is sitting on a D. Stark wagon with Arthur Foster. They are outside the rear of Eden Terrace, Shiney Row, in 1970.

John and Kenneth Stark marking out the foundations of Foundry Farm House in 1972. The farm became Stark's depot.

John and Kenneth Stark at their depot in later years. John is on the left.

Entertainment

Two photographs of Penshaw Community Association Pantomimes from the mid 1970s. On the left is a production of Sleeping Beauty with Ellen Faith (on chair) and Anne Charlton with two Wombles – very popular at that time. On the right photograph is Alma Howe (née Wilson) – sitting on the stage far left – who was the producer for the pantomimes.

A production of the pantomime Dick Whittington at Penshaw Community Association. Included in the photograph are: Sheila Charlton, Jean Chapman, Joan Harrison (the cat), Ella Jackson, Margaret Mole, Elsie Lumsden, Gordon Chapman, George Lumsden and Thora Thompson.

Right: Another Penshaw Community Association pantomime. Included are: Alan Charlton, Lesley Shale, Jean Chapman, Margaret Mole and Elsie Lumsden.

Left: Here is a Penshaw Community Association celebration to commemorate the Second World War. Local ladies take part in this song.

The Community Association is still going strong and in September 2010 organised the Scarecrow Trail around the village – organised by Pat Hart.

Right: 'Meet the gang 'cos the boys are here ... the boys to entertain you!' The men take part in the show at Penshaw Community Association to remember those who served in the Second World War. This sketch was inspired by the popular TV comedy series – 'It Ain't Half Hot Mum' – based on an army entertainment troupe during the war.

Winter Time

Above: A gentleman clearing heavy snow fall in a back street of Shiney Row in the winter of 1941.

Clearing The Snow

My husband's first job, after we came back from Birmingham at the end of Second World War, was in 1947 when we had very bad snow. The snow blocked the road leading from Penshaw to Sunderland. Norman was on the dole at that time and had to sign on. All the local men on unemployment benefit where sent to clear the snow – so they had a job of sorts! It took quite a while to clear all the snow because it was very deep. Norman eventually got a job at the Birtley Munitions Works.

In The Bleak Mid Winter

In living memory the harshest winters were in 1941, 1947 and 1963. In the winter of 1940/41 the temperature dropped to ten degrees below freezing on Wearside on the night of the 20th January. In February 1941 snow fell continually for three days. All this terrible weather and the war was on!

In 1947 local streets were covered in snow from late January to mid March. February saw some of the lowest average daily temperatures recorded in the century. In the years after the war there was also fuel rationing and power cuts at this time.

The bad weather in 1963 started on the 2nd January with a three day blizzard. The icy weather continued until the thaw finally came in March.

The snowy conditions experienced at the beginning of 2010 seem like nothing compared to these really harsh winters.

James Jefferson, pigeon fancier, with his crees covered by heavy snow in the gardens just off Penshaw Village.

Above: By a lane leading to Penshaw Hill are Ellen Guthrie, her mother Nellie and Rex the dog.

Left: Penshaw Hill covered in a blanket of snow. Ellen Guthrie is in the foreground.

The Harsh Winter of 1947

I had never seen so much snow in my life as I did in the winter of 1947. Both me and my husband were out of work at that time and on the 'dole'. We were living in Garden Place, Penshaw, at that time, and I had to sign on at Herrington Burn. I didn't think I would ever get to the dole office in the snow. There was no transport running and I had to walk. I was very lucky because someone had walked down to Herrington Burn before me and left their footprints. So the easiest way to cope in the snow was to put my feet into these footprints and I eventually got to where I needed to go – and back home as well!

Women's Groups

Above: The Sisterhood of the Old Methodist Chapel. Included are: Mrs Kerry, Mrs Watson, Mrs Jefferson, Mrs Anderson, Mrs Hall, Mrs Young, Mrs Wallace and Mrs Darvel.

Left: Margaret Jane Ramshaw known as Peggy, who lives in Shiney Row, was born in 1923. She was a founder member of Philadelphia Ladies' Club. Peggy was the Secretary for nineteen years and then Chairman for many years after that. She is still a member today. When the club celebrated their 50th birthday in 2008, Peggy cut the cake.

Members of Shiney Row Women's Institute – formed in 1933.

The ladies of St John's Church, Shiney Row, in the 1950s.

Members of Shiney Row Women's Institute. This photograph was taken during their 21st birthday celebrations in 1954.

Bobby Thompson

Left: A postcard of Penshaw Staiths near Fatfield. This community has now gone and the area is known as Mount Pleasant. The biggest claim to fame for Penshaw Staiths is that it was the birth place of one of the North East's most famous characters – the comedian Bobby Thompson

PHONE CHESTER-LE-STREET 2210.

Bobby Thompson

Comedian

CLEAN AND CLEVER "WOT CHEOR GEORDIE" FAME

ALL COMS. :- PHYLLIS THOMPSON,
25, LOEFIELD,
GREAT LUMLEY, CHESTER-LE-STREET.

Right: Bobby Thompson's business card when he lived at Great Lumley. It says he is 'Clean and Clever' and also he is from 'Wot Cheor Geordie Fame'. Bobby, with his trademark flat cap, scruffy jumper and cigarette always in his mouth, toured the clubs of the North East – known affectionately as 'The Little Waster.'

Wot Cheor Geordie was the popular BBC programme featuring local comedians.

Left: The cover of Bobby Thompson's album – 'The Little Waster'. His jokes and stories of everyday life were very popular and when this album was released it was one of the best selling records in the North East.

Bobby was born at 4 The Staiths, Penshaw in 1911. His father was a deputy at North Biddick Colliery. Both of his parents died when he was a boy and he lived with his sisters – first at Fatfield and later at New Penshaw. At school he got the nickname 'Little Tonka'. He started work at North Biddick Colliery at the age of fourteen. In 1931 he left the pit to work in show business.

Along The River

North Biddick Colliery near the Victoria Viaduct. At the start of the twentieth century the pit employed around 350 men and boys but by the 1930s it had been closed. A ferry operated near to the Viaduct for men from the Penshaw area who worked at the colliery who needed to cross the river.

Right: The Alice Well at Cox Green in 2010. Its inscription is starting to fade but you can just see 'Rebuilt in 1895.' This well was the only source of water for the area up until 1947. The well is believed to have a connection with Lewis Carroll and his books *Alice's Adventures in Wonderland* and *Through The Looking Class*. The author was a visitor to the area in the nineteenth century.

A postcard view of the River Wear, with Penshaw Monument in the background, at Fatfield. A mother poses with two children and a wonderful old pram just before the First World War.

In this 2010 photograph the trees obscure the view of the river but Penshaw Monument can still be seen in the distance.

An atmospheric photograph of a train steaming over the Victoria Viaduct – named for the Coronation of Queen Victoria. The bridge was first opened for traffic in 1839. Between the arches can be seen North Biddick Colliery.

The Victoria Viaduct in 2010. The colliery and trains are now gone. The last train across was in 1993.

Fatfield Bridge from Worm Hill. This was a postcard sent in 1922. Although some claim the Lambton Worm wrapped itself around Penshaw Hill, as many people believe the legend belongs to Worm Hill.

The view from Worm Hill in 2010. There are new houses in the distance beyond Fatfield Bridge but the building at the bottom of the hill – the Biddick Inn – remains.

Cox Green Footbridge, opened in 1958. In the distance is Washington Chemical Works.

Cox Green Footbridge in 2010. The Chemical Works have gone and the area has returned to a much more rural place.

Herrington Burn

A postcard of Herrington Burn from 1920s. This postcard was produced by the Gateshead photographer Robert Johnston and was taken on the same day as the picture of the Tivoli Cinema on the top of the facing page.

Herrington Burn in 2010. The trams have gone and now this spot is the site of a busy roundabout.

A postcard the Tivoli Cinemas at Herrington Burn. This was the local cinema for many from Penshaw and Shiney Row. The Tivoli is advertising a number of films – one of them is 'Tarzan of the Apes.' This postcard was sent to London and the message on the back is typical of the period. Some of it reads: 'We had rain Thursday morning but it was nice and warm in the afternoon, it is not very warm this morning but perhaps when the sun comes out it will be better. We are going to Roker on Saturday with the Sunday school if it does not rain.'

In 2010 the cinema has gone and replaced by flats called Tivoli Buildings.

Shiney Row Male Voice Choir

In 2009 Shiney Row Male Voice Choir celebrated its Golden Jubilee with a number of events. One of those special occasions was a celebrity concert on 25th April 2009 at Ewesley Road Methodist Church in Sunderland. The programme told of the choir's early history:

"On 15th May 1959, a meeting was held in the school-room of Station Road Methodist Church, Shiney Row, at which the male section of the Church Choir decided to increase their number by inviting men from other churches to join them. Ten men were present, and donations were given, totalling £1, to buy music.

A year later, at the Annual Meeting, 21 members were present and the balance in hand was reported as a healthy £7 and a penny ha'penny. At this meeting, it was decided to hold an Annual Concert, establishing the tradition of inviting professional guest soloist to sing at Annual "Celebrity" Concerts which has been maintained ever since, with many soloists of international repute having being pleased to come and sing with Shiney Row."

The programme of the Choir's Golden Jubilee Celebrity Concert in 2009.

Shiney Row Male Voice Choir during their Golden Jubilee year of 2009.

Days To Remember

An autogiro taking part in Cobham's Air Show at Burnmoor in the 1930s. An autogiro was an early helicopter – a very rare sight in the 1930s. Penshaw Monument is in the distance.

Sir Alan Cobham was a pilot in the Royal Flying Corps (which later became the RAF) during the First World War and was an early pioneer of long distance flights. In the early 1930s he set up the National Aviation Day displays that became known as Cobham's Flying Circus. A team of pilots and their aeroplanes toured the country giving most people their first experience of seeing a plane up close. Displays such as this between the two world wars were known as 'barnstormers'. Cobham's shows visited established air fields but often set down on local fields as they did when they came to Burnmoor in the 1930s.

Cobham's Flying Circus came to an end in 1935 and Sir Alan went on to have a distinguished career in the aviation industry. He died in 1973.

Exciting Times

When I was a child I went to see the Cobham airshow. Cobham landed at Primrose Hill near Burnmoor – the field opposite the Dun Cow pub. In those days it was open fields – there is a housing estate there now. To go and see an aeroplane in the 1930s was a big thing. We got up close to the plane and it was a great thrill for everyone. I thought Cobham was a good man. He was travelling around the country to different areas. I was just a youngster at the time. He drew a very big crowd and I struggled to get near to the aeroplane. I wanted to touch a plane but I didn't get near enough. We were sorry that he wasn't in our area longer. Not many people at that time had seen an aeroplane close up. We'd seen them in the sky but to get close to them and to meet the pilots who flew them was exciting.

An Air Raid Precaution group at Shiney Row, 1941 Back row: Joe Lewes, George Richardson, Fletcher, Rutter, Nightingdale, Mustard. Front row: Mary Lowery, Mary Tubman, E. Snowdon, D. MacFarlane, Edna Brown.

The wedding of Denis Strafford and Freda Todd at St Oswald's Church, Shiney Row on 17th September 1949.

Happy times on Penshaw Hill in the snow. Some of these youngsters have some pretty fancy sledges. The ones in my day were a lot more basic – but just as fun.

A Wartime Christmas

Christmas during the Second World War was very different from today. Money was scarce and people were worried about the war – you were losing friends and family members to the conflict. There was of course a lot of pressure on people who were serving in the forces – the soldiers, airmen and sailors.

It was very peaceful at my husband's mother's house where we were staying. She did manage a Christmas cake which she made herself. But we couldn't go to town and enjoy it as you would on a ordinary time – it was very subdued.

Maureen Strafford, Band Major in Burnmoor Coldstreamers around 1967. Bands were very popular in the 1960s and '70s.

Also available from Summerhill Books

Thanks For The Memories
Fence Houses, Lambton, Burnmoor, Chilton Moor, Dubmire & Bankhead

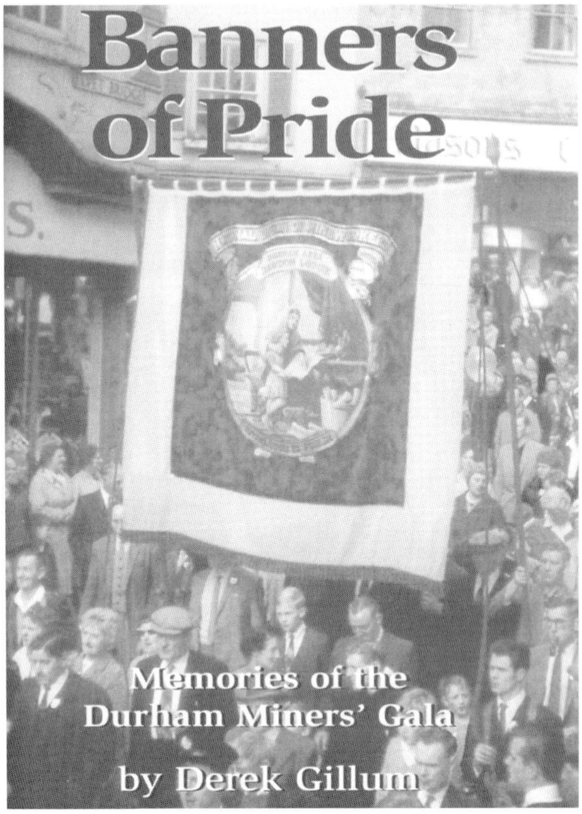

Banners of Pride
Memories of the Durham Miners' Gala

Summerhill Books

Summerhill Books publishes local history books in Northumberland, Durham and Tyneside.

To receive a free catalogue send a SAE envelope to:

Summerhill Books
PO Box 1210, Newcastle NE99 4AH

or email:
summerhillbooks@yahoo.co.uk

or visit our website to view the full range of titles

www.summerhillbooks.co.uk

Postage and packaging is FREE for all UK orders.

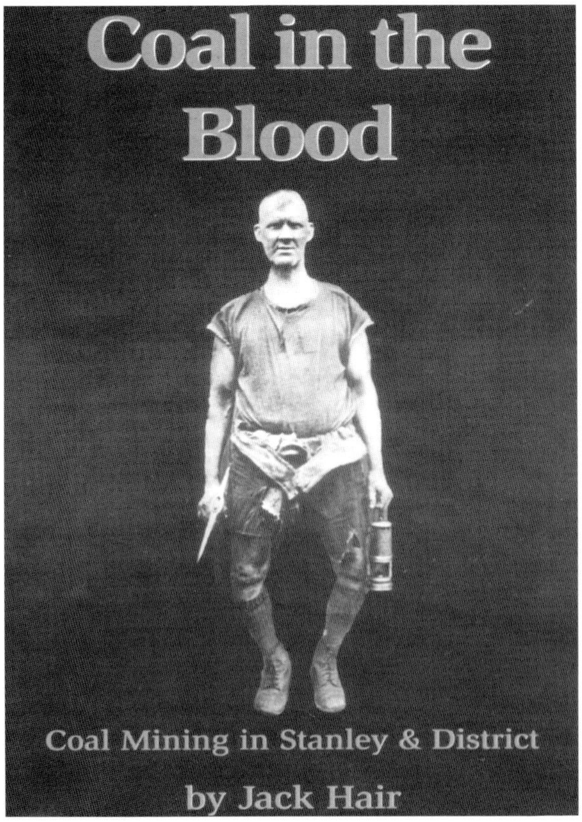

Coal in The Blood
Coal Mining in Stanley & District